Nomad

Nomad

Poems on
Human Origins

Paul Mills

SMOKE STACK BOOKS

Smokestack Books
1 Lake Terrace, Grewelthorpe, Ripon HG4 3BU
e-mail: info@smokestack-books.co.uk
www.smokestack-books.co.uk

ISBN 978-1-9163121-9-7

Smokestack Books
is represented
by Inpress Ltd

for Keith,
Michael, Matt
and Leila

Contents

**Part One
The Gates
of Grief**

History etc

a boy with a book   turning the pages
The Story of the British People in Pictures

Mary facing the block with scaffold composure
Queen Jane blindfold over straw

the gunpowder plot conspirators
And when did you last see your father?

a boy stands in the dock
about to be hanged   accused of theft
staring into the eyes of the criminal code

later Nelson   not much older
saying goodbye to his distraught mother

SLAVES on an auctioneer's billboard
a Paris street   a woman beating a drum

history as error and correction

The King and Kaiser in a carriage
then   *The spark that set the world alight*
finally   A *record breaking train*

we lived in a semi in a cul-de-sac
in the middle of Cheshire in the fifties

the co-op by the railway bridge sold Hovis
my father umpired the second eleven

I was in the church choir   we got a dog
my mother's rice puddings were awful

history it seemed wasn't interested
in a time and place without events

we watched General Montgomery on film
shot by shot the ricochet of artillery

when did it start?

turning the pages back and further back
there were scenes of people in their moment

how with a puzzled look muscular savages
urged a stone the weight of a railway carriage
uphill to Stonehenge on wheels of logs

while before that a man in skins
sat carving an object out of bone
there on rock the outline of a horse

a woman   a man   he with bow and arrow
wandered about hopelessly in the cold

if only they could have climbed on board
got away on a record-breaking train
all of them missing out on *now*

the boy wondered if any of them were fearful
like Nelson's mother
but they knew nothing   weren't even British
lost somewhere in the struggle against ice

and before that and before that
there were others   but who?   where?
in a story beginning with no story

Quarry Caves, Dorset

teams of men wielding picks
quarried rock carried by carts

up a rutted white road to the village
or by sea to Poole   London

for the building of monuments   cathedrals
sea-smell oozes from walls

under a stone some wriggling thing
our ancestor and inheritor

sketched by the bright sun on upright rock
a tap-dance figure from music-hall

shares its likeness with a Picasso horse
in a cavort out of the last century

while Ariadne hands Theseus a thread
by which he might find his way

bringing the Minotaur's head
from the Jurassic

shapes like loose pelts   anvils
cubist versions of square

surfaces a pallet knife might smooth
pitted by shadow

flint   chert   limestone
astral upholstery

rays from its star falling aslant
one afternoon on a chance planet

Timelines

room to room you travel the world
downward to its beginnings
no life older than stromatolites
on sea-bottom rocks grainy as braille

blood-bathed hungers   ferns that swim
something like a pineapple with a mouth

then up again   and the eye of an ichthyosaur
trapped in lias   muscle-ringed for power vision
catches you as you pass

to surface in Anthropology   chips of flint
with found or made edges
one knapped around the fossil of a shell

masks that glare through glass towards
an opposite tiled wall
each one a stopped clock

this totem pole three storeys high
should be gazing out across the Pacific
beaks and wings now husks   its spirits flown

over the road is a John Lewis store cafe
the place to eat   lettering in grey across one wall

the year our founder took the first step
from visionary thought to innovative business
Byron born on the same site as our store in Oxford Street

then one by Betjeman
if the end of the world should come
I'd like to be in a haberdashery department
nothing unpleasant could ever happen there

top floor windows
aged complexions
city roofs and spires

from hunter-killers of the Cretaceous
to   *opens branches in the Channel Islands*
who you are is always when and where

In the sky with diamonds

shouting to me from the gully
he'd found a scapula
femur   parts of a skull
that moment when we said *hominid*
jumping about and howling
in the hundred-degree heat

driving back   my thumb on the horn
afterwards beers   discussion all round
erect walking   tool use   food sharing
brain enlargement   so much high-school
top-of-the-heap bravado   and the song
playing all night

he named her   sky-high with it
she's as far back as we've got
3.2 million years   so now   because
of that bright morning one November
the history of prehistory will be different
her bones in his safe

footprints in volcanic ash
some type of early human group
unpromising when you speculate
but still   the mystery of sources
mud and silt washed down
by new young rivers   layers of a cake

and on top   fragments   a few hard
factual chunks   and us   thinking they fit
knuckle to socket   the whole story
ready to get up and walk

run and print the dust   or that's the hope
some too scattered even to be lost

I'm flying home   trying to locate her
australopithecus   not yet *habilis*
tracking invisible points of shift
cello music on my cassette
each passage of notes a slow legato
as we approach the glittering East River

Song without words

deep in the throat   in the chest
a breathing in the knees   through the feet

soon the whole body hums and dances
voices swaying together without words

a circle no predator can approach
hummed soft in the miles of savannah grass

The story of hands

hands got so far off the ground
they forgot about making footprints
faces studied them carefully
what could we do with these?   what could we not?

thumbs moved upward to join fingers
closed on flint in pits of chipping and clattering
stone seemed the point but pointed where?

after so many hundred thousand years
hands were restless
wandered adrift between holes in flutes
left their image upright on cave rock

feeling the weight of boredom in the palm
got it together   shook on it

arrow-shafts   antler-bone   ivory
planed   sharpened   burned   bound
signing this way over there stop quietly
more and more animals died

spears   pruning hooks   on and on
hands drawing metal out of stone
tearing down   refashioning
making things that make things

hands close to exhaustion   *how are we different*
they wondered   *from first-evolved hands?*
tiny hurricane finger-whorls through the leaves
in no time driven to clicking words
tapping information   and what next?

sometimes the forward gaze of the face lost interest
so that hands again did what they wanted

hands of a woman playing with those of a baby in a railway
carriage
the long explore of lovers' hands filling themselves with each
other

and sometimes hands were lost for words
hands laid on coffins   hands where they can't help

Quick brown eyes with something like consciousness

when the sun`s heat collapses in woods near what will become
                                                      Thetford
when your only retreat from the night wind is your own skin

when the sky is draughty and leaks rain
when children are born in the shadow of frost

if your mind could begin to compete with the drifting of blowing
                                                               ice
if the sound in your throat could warn of the avalanche

if dry land could be launched and floated somehow
if the deer would run again into the valley of lightning-torched
                                                            grass

because words like glassy and air-conditioning
are a thousand centuries in the future

if the baby soon to be crowned by its mother will breathe and cry
if this piece of rock could cut

if wild milk wild honey and wild grass could somehow be tamed
if the beasts of the field could be harvested

if the dripping ram`s throat could appease your anger against God
if you could only find the instructions for chloroform

if home is a charcoal scar in a desert   where are your friends?
why don`t you pray for them to intervene   write them a letter?

tell them you stand speechless at the table
trapped in the finished past

The dead who have gone down into deep time

this small dinosaur skeleton on a shelf
in the Museum of Earth Sciences in Cambridge

its hands extended blind as if feeling for something
as if flicking away little drops of water

the head poised   about to conduct   steadying the orchestra
quite unwilling to turn in our direction

designed   it seems so carefully   like a fern
bones like branches intercepted by wind

surely   when it evolved   some sense of beauty
must have declared itself   *because I am   this is*
look no further

 balanced so finely   the whole arrangement
stretched out like Asia   like a drawing

a season in hell of course   the music of screams
and soon after the first fossils appeared here behind glass

for William and Dorothy   apostrophists of the earth
rocks and trees were already almost events

a child-sized hill of moss   an old thorn bush
that moment on the lake when the mountain moved

towards him through a dream of still-living darkness
as if the earth were trying to become a story

the dead who have gone down into deep time
starting to come back   beautiful and bone-swift

The Gates of Grief

a couple of gods were talking about creation
bringing back existence step by step

first   creatures with faces like cutlery
flesh-torn bones scattered
yet they remember only the heat of joy
threads of desire in the wind   seeds of the forest
one curled up continent of them both
a single green landmass from the Red Sea to the Andes

there were complications   for instance   magma
bonding and splitting   the chemistry of furnaces
they saw fractures deepening into seas
Antarctica's flux separating the Capes
O my America   he whispered
while she watched India crash into Asia

at last   at rest in the midst of it all   Africa
Somalia's brow-ridge staring east
long dangling-forward face
from Eritrea to Swaziland

the waters of Chad   Africa's ear-drum
listened to wind in sand   the clank of geese
howling and slithering of cries becoming silence
then one new cry like a bone needle
a persistence threading breath to breath

together they looked down at the thing born
there had been others   skulls like turrets
sounds in the mouth an endless chewing
unable to make words

after all those variants of ape
this one gives me hope   she said   listen
when it cries   the silences of Africa recede
don't let's waste the chance but go with it
                              see where it goes
maybe it will mend the seams we can't

the Great Rift Valley pointed blank
at the easiest crossing-place into Asia
as if geology had desired it
a gateway where the between-sea narrowed

and all it took to start the world
was a tiny tremor in the brain   shifting the gaze
so that elsewhere fissured into distances you could reach

                    remember   he's saying

let's go back to that moment when I turned
to you as we watched them make the crossing
two hundred of them   fathers and mothers
of everyone now alive

if we could be there   say those words again
when it was all to come   all in the air   monkey temples
stories in glass   tracks   roads   gunfire   crematoria
building it   knocking it down   building it again

will it be worth it? I asked   and you said yes

Why an albatross feeds plastic to its young

two million years and a restless hand picks up a raw pebble
not yet shaped   knobbed and heavy enough
to crush bone for the marrow

less far back and the hand this time
runs an edge along a thumb   doesn't just use it   throw it away
but thinks   wait   use this to make another and another

sparse scatterings of tribes differently human
moving over a rough un-angled surface
what will be Europe   Asia   rocky plains

pointlessly long invisible slow progress   what held them back?
were they hearing inklings   wary of future
that first whispering   *thou shalt not*   of paradise?

time locked in wastes behind the brow   in the pure air
days and nights un-calendared   stars above them alive

Earth still to be used   not yet edged   not yet split and edged
not yet shaped   not yet fitting into their hands

The fix

is to shape stones that bite   sharp as incisors
under a carob's shade   among wild rubble
seeing the wide plain   the herds of bison

is not to scavenge but become hunters
is to make death happen where you want it
is to make the clouds of vultures wait

a world shaped by fix   the power of fix
not this of uninterrupted heat
not wind   ice   but shelter and fire

is to invent needles   invent furrows
join strong hands to flexible minds
is to make them restless for completion

on my hearth a poker shaped to a point
iron-handled shovel   iron tongs
sawn logs   at my back a radiator   hot

in my freezer a package of lamb   ice
salmon   broccoli   bread   it's everywhere
we live by the fix   will die from it probably

yet I also notice what's not the fix
on the mantle-piece a peculiar jug
striped Navaho sphere-thing from Nevada

here a guitar   paintings   patterns   games
saying to me the fix isn't all   never was
there is the fix held back   the fix in reverse

coins and swords flung to the waters   other rhythms
saying however far you reach you hear it
hear them both   the fix and not the fix

Looking at a hand-axe

to see it you have to hold it
palm gripping the curve
thumb towards tip

point and edge
shaped for use
to slice hack pierce

dents for fingers
squeeze it
smooth wouldn't do

you can look now
at its symmetry
an exact bi-face

laid flat
under this desk lamp
delta-winged

aimed   its reach global
ready for take-off
seductive

not becoming extinct
until the millennia
it travelled found it so

From the Palaeolithic

dawn frost   the heating on
and condensation already formed on the kitchen's inside glass
beginning to slide   trickle in loops
spirals   spurs   wriggling forest vines   and a figure
between branches   climbing out   coming through
hauling himself forward into a clearing

I've seen him before   imagined him
one of the first coming into Europe
out of the east following rivers and sunsets
climbing a peak of rocks above the Danube

he stands in the dripping pane looking around him
testing the view where rafts are working upstream

generations after him will reach ice
will they survive the ferocities of the tundra?
he is one of the first sons of the mother who is our mother
he will never be rich   never be poor

through him   behind him   my garden
beginning to shine   an apple tree where a wren flits

how far will his thoughts carry him?
in his domed skull are all the tools he'll need
to survive in paradise and demolish it
come no further   I ought to say   *go back!*

he faces me   between pathways of water
will he begin to melt when the frost melts?
he is disfiguring now in the heat of the kitchen

divers reaching a deep recess will find his skull
scattered among bones of cave bears

The story of a line

when did it start   the urge to intrude
on spaces   move forward some small mark?

one like this slate engraving of a seal
brought overland to the upper Rhine
token of wanderings   who was who
from where   as the cold roared

daubed mollusc shell
somewhere in Africa   deep in the stem
of the mind
ostrich egg the size of a baby's skull
painted with feathers
a line twice the age ever thought
for marks   landmarks

then across bone   ivory
carved by points   and here
just millennia from ourselves
so close we almost remember   it leaps
leaps   is a gazelle
is a bison's black elastic stride on a cave wall

how from that to lines drawn by ploughs
track-ways   roads
marks of excursions into a future

and this morning   near the confluence
of the Célé and Lot   travelling West
in the early blue
an attack of vapour trails   more and more
how they come on!
Toulouse   London   New York

once though were a feathery touch
untraceable   folded up
in the all-dark   in the drift

Eastern Siberia to Tierra del Fuego

smoke blown from fires in the granite rocks
white mountains sheer as broken-off pieces
                              of frozen ocean

migrations through the degrees of steppe-tundra
thousands-strong herds of moving antlers
still just enough lichen

people didn't know that with each step
already they were changing east into west
here at the top of the Pacific

they had with them what they could do
with stone points   canoes
what they knew about stars   ice
reindeer and bone needles

the coast steered them south
a long igneous spine twisted
this way and that but kept going
after the fiery cold of an ice desert
every day the sun was a hot spring
here in the back country of paradise

alone and not alone   there were ghosts
the dead   so easily offended
must be abandoned

there were spirits   stories of spirits
sun   moon   adulterous twilight
there was the wind and the other wind lifting
                              hairs along your skin
voices that whispered under your skin

two thousand years   a long journey
and when they arrived Thames still flowed north
                                    into the Arctic
people in England were drinking from human skulls

while scattered along this ragged outstretched wing-tip
                                    of America
they lived on with carefully risked persistence
until certain ships came down from Europe
to the almost landless south

1832

Charles Darwin   aged 26   feels the crossover tides slip
under the cabin floor to the Southern Ocean
if only he'd stayed in Good Success Bay
not sailed west   set foot on land   he can't sleep
in his journal he records swarms of butterflies
                                    blown out to sea
Ehrenberg's paper on phosphorescence
speculates on extinct species   giant armadillos   capybaras
none of it can distract him

instead he sees their little ship like a map illustration
inching towards the Pacific
its sails caught in a storm straight off the mountain
lashed by the spinal tail of the Cordilleras
he speaks directly now into his journal   remembering
at the sea's edge   *those most miserable of creatures*
a naked woman and her child   streaks of sleet
on her breast and the baby's skin

what are they doing here in his century?   Europe   America
slipping past him into some closed ravine
a thicket of gestures   painted grimaces
men   if they were men   asleep on wet leaves
here on this final landmass to be peopled
their future appears to him like their past   abject
a long steep-sided sound   from end to end
swallowed by cloud   no *improvement*
no point in thought except to chip at limpets

Shadow-time

flying from Guangzhou to Amsterdam
after obscure hollows of black Siberia
the plane noses south over St Petersburg

points of tiny concentrated light
show up as roads
then fade to a blur that's not quite day

could still be forest   could still be
pre ice-age people down there
near one of the last of the rivers to freeze

imagine them in the half-rubbed-out dark
our flight path at the edge of dissolving night
                    in prolonged dawn

not far below the rushing of cabin air
shadow-defined ridges   troughed valleys
minds still unmapped

in their sky just silences   birds   thunder
before we came leaving trails to vaporise

Supernatural

as when a loved child walks unhurt from a burning forest
into your open arms yet it's not her
or a long growl lichen-haired
mixes its breathing with the familiar

or some new thought is interrupted
by the disturbed voice of a dead mother
by a surge in the air of a lost brother
the dead come back   try to see through your eyes

look look   they say   at some lovely thing
a green fir cone   a jumping fish   they see it
or when I'm playing a flute   one they made
so we hear their singing clustering with us

or the voice of a caribou skin
as I cut and loosen it from the body
saying *like this like this   do it like this*
look how I give you myself still warm

but sometimes not   sometimes fire won't talk
sparks into nothing   into wind that howls just to itself
sometimes I know only my own hands
that the only skill in them is mine

I hear roaring out of the dead steppe
on and on and on   to the air   the stars
to where rock is rock   flayed by ice
and so raise my cry to the ancestors   *come*

tell us how to survive the dark
so we can crouch together by a fire
no strangeness in their flickering faces
feeling in its heat the desired lost

On the Eurasian plain

there had been others glimpsed vanishing
in and out of the forest   but it was these who thrived
ice making the air dry   holding their future to it

year by year the weight they had to haul themselves against
grew heavier   every day heavier   testing their grip
a long horizon sweeping them with its wind

sweeping away trees so they had to learn to hunt in the open
following groups of caribou   aurochs   mammoth
for their blood-energy
herds shifting over the steppe-tundra
as they too shifted with hides for tents   bones for tent-poles
bones not wood for fires

homeless tribes   a sea of ice deepening around them
some moved west   some east
the land trackless desert   finding their way
through it   against it   the weight of it day and night
hauling them forward
without knowledge other than how to be
how to keep warm   food water shelter   how to continue

not knowing that their becoming would become ours
asking how they lived   little to go on
when it was they learned to sew with bone
how they ever found a way to think
perhaps hope   sense there was a story
in that wind howling without a breath
talk to each other

begin to carve   in some off-guard moment
this solid form of mammoth ivory
hold it as a counterweight for ballast
joy meaning touch   in the otherwise waste

Nomad

you following herds followed by wolves
to where the sun a red flare

holds open a space between cloud and tundra
your own fires making extinct tracks

through boreal forest
not knowing you've crossed a quarter of the globe

out from behind the curve of it   slanting west

roads and towns of the Swabian Alb invisible
in the future

following new-melted tons of Lone and Danube

wing-beat and honk of night-flying geese
croak of ravens   eagle talons sliding out of the air

a long-thriving hunger swallowing you
some child-voice in you with its cry

bringing the wounded man   the lame woman

cold still weakening your grip   startling you
into exhausted numbness   driving you

closer towards each other's furious resolve
that no life possible must be lost

Where only fire can see

a polar door opens in the Ardeche
letting through warm winds from the south

spring coming so that the ground shines
under bare branches

mass and heft of shoulders and flanks
hooves scraping and stamping

all of it lit by heat in your own skin
and by torches as you go underground

into the hidden
lifting cave shadows   hearing a thought

brush your fire on rock to keep it alight
then pick up these little bits of charcoal

among hand-prints   clawings of bears

new marks in the recesses
a scribble that is antler   another

with one sweep spine flank shoulder neck eye
forms overlapping   entangled together

lions   horses   curving the rock
into being out of your own making

the cold returns
but with a new thing seen
without beauty no survival

**Part Two
Gatherings
and close-ups**

Just So Stories

the cat that walked by itself through the wet wild woods
the woman's magic of the clean mutton
shoulder-bone in the firelight
stories of how the world first slipped from chaos
the crab that played with the sea's hollows
huge and moving awkwardly

my mother's voice reading was drawing a net
strange places and creatures spilling from it
squirming and alive with other existence
slithering back away from us but named in their cold element

I kept asking for the one about a butterfly
who lifted the palace of King Suleiman-Bin-Daoud
a thousand miles in the air by stamping its foot
conjuring djinns and affrits at the same moment
as the king twisted a magic ring on his finger
how he and his favourite queen devised this plan
frightening his angry wives and the butterfly's wife to a hush

did Kipling like women?   I knew nothing
of the sexual history of quarrelling
only that things with wings the size of a city
raised it high in the air by its four corners
setting it down again with complete precision
exactly where it was because of a butterfly

I didn't know that my mother's voice was lifting us both
gently above the anger she felt inside her
so that the words hushed her as she read them

Kathleen

my mother's sister is very old now and I'm talking to her
as she lies in bed in the nursing home
remembering with me as I remember   the house
where my grandparents lived   where she grew up
a cobbled street up-hill as the view widened
gas works   viaduct   road at the top

front door   side gate   and the garden I tell her
blackcurrant bushes   tarred shed roof   kitchen step
uneven yard   then the parlour
tinny upright I pounded   living-room hearth where
she   third eldest   rationing at its height
let slip a full half-pound of butter into the fire

I tell her this story just as I was told it as a child
as we move on together room to room
the three-cornered staircase   hall   curtain pole
open door where they crowded   grown-up girls
the day their brother Jack came home from the war

'Rene!' Kathleen calls out to my mother
to the space by the bed 'are you hearing this?'
it stopped me a minute   things in the house
meat safe   sideboard   present and not
memory like some old adhesive in a drawer
doors that go on opening in a house you never leave

so my dead mother is with us as we talk
their mother too is listening   when Kathleen asks
if I've seen them recently   her mother   father
her brother Jack   or maybe I am Jack she thinks
or her father   or a minute ago Rene was here
she isn't deceived

1966

me and my friends building fires   I'd nearly forgotten
faces moving in thought or speaking or laughing

acting attitudes   singing with a guitar   being ourselves
or outside ourselves   together by an estuary or the sea

I've seen it too in woods   at the edges of towns
remains of fires   gathering-places   in use probably at night

youth   driftwood   wave-break   voices
the story of the future not yet cast   still to unfold
innocent of event

a circle of heated stones   the wind's charred edge

a world beginning or ending   it was the same
out of our hands   or a way through in reach   just possible
the weathering sky still calm

paradise found in some illusion of starting again all over

Looking for America

you try to catch somewhere being America
the scent of hot dry air   of fresh anchovies

or when a buzzard soars so long and high
you think of forest pinnacles then blue jays

their quick-sliding chack-chack   but you're in France
where TV sets aren't tilted by earthquakes

you heard about the Monterey peninsula and
Salinas Valley shifting inches in a minute and a half
while Wales hasn't trembled in a hundred years

as for those fuzzy hills of the north in Cumbria
you look for big sweeps of new rock
the planet growing straight up out of itself

Zabriski Point   or leaking its core fire into Mono Lake
the whole state burning off in a haze

women smiling at you with cold warm eyes
proud to be owned and free   themselves and yours

you want one more overnight drive to the sun
places named simply by what's found there

Boulder Creek   Lone Pine   Coconut Grove
diners by what you eat   Zannotto's Pasta
Tortilla Flats   by who cooks   Gayle's Rosticceria.

you want to find it just like that first time
loving the mountain roadside scent
of fennel and crushed eucalyptus

Ansel Adams

I think of him as a boy on his own
by the sea at Lobos Creek
the Golden Gate raising its abstracts
among shipwrecks and landslides

down on Baker Beach   jumping from boulders
before learning the piano kept him indoors
bit him with its arithmetic

the earthquake   more than just weather underground
flung him against a wall and broke his nose

when he grew up
Yosemite glanced at him and he gazed back
his fingers couldn't keep still

somebody put a camera in them
each direction of strike
timed by the eye   now   now

I imagine him   an older brother
the one I never had   running so fast
I couldn't catch him
leaping along that shore   pianist   photographer

I have one of his prints on a bedroom wall
rocks in thousands slanted by movements of clouds
the rubble of the planet
exactness in the grip of unfinished shaping

Anaviapik

is drawing a map in the snow like somebody speaking
to somebody who is lost
not quite sure of the way through the wide pass
and so we set off   tea   sugar   in our minds
the seals we'll kill   keeping starvation away but it's there
travelling with us   a near-by horizon of sea ice broken up
where seals should be   slabs   fractures
boulders we climb where the sledges get trapped   continue

slow hard hours follow
we build a snow-house
eat the last of our meat
there's no dark only a thinning brightness
instead of dawn we wake to a storm
the dogs crouched very low have become drifts
we head for the shore and a drift that will make bricks
another snow-house   another lapse
of daylight we call night
no meat   just biscuits and the little jets of the stove

heading out again across the fjord
eight or nine hours of deepening snow   jokes   laughter
stop again   eating boiled ears from caribou skins
no breathing holes   no seals
Anaviapik says we must ration our sugar   one spoon each
you look so thin I say to him   his face all bone and jaw-line
he says we probably won't make it back

I hadn't known   hadn't thought of the risk
no one had tried to hope or give up hope
each day the same joking and friendly silence

the wind coming across from a hidden place
a gap nothing can close off or block out
we find a hut   light the stove
Anaviapik finds checkers some hunters left
seal-meat in a cache   we're all set up
the dogs are fed   he moves his hand across the squares
we laugh   every day he teaches me his language
not just words but how to become Inuit

Climb

for Tom Mills

beautiful day   the clouds
a slow-moving pavement above the moors
here it's full blue and he must think
immediately   think now
how to relieve the weight
of his body pinned there   that small graze
far up is a ledge but invisible almost
what could be scratchings from ice-fields
line the face in extended webs
otherwise hardly a mark
but must do something   needs
rhythm   and with one push that seems
unplanned he's higher   hangs by a finger
high over a drop that could be fatal
a crack thin as a line   almost not there
moves again   finds friction for a grip
this rock his only place to be
infinite blank face which he climbs
intimately   in twenty thousand years
its big-lidded overhang hasn't shifted
he's hugging it from below
then is on the top   how did he do that?
stands now on the sky saying yes a lot

Professor Lu

is a collector of framed liquid geologies
this one   she says   Xiaomin translating
isn't it perfectly that Ayatollah   cheekbone
and jaw   jagged expression   surely?

an art of rolling and grinding   dark igneous
ice wedging   great heats   but Professor Lu
likes likenesses   is adamant   so we comply
Ivan the Terrible?   I say   *waterfalls maybe?*

she smiles   still pale with welcome
suffering a little   the one by the table
where we sit eating lotus roots
is a waterfall certainly   and paddy fields

groups of women harvesting   a lake
though I see force-fields happening
like thoughts in a scanned brain
obscure to us

and think of the drawings of Wen Zhengming
little bushes   polite figures sitting among folds
of inchoate rock   as she pours tea
landslides from an earthquake on her TV

Under Jade Dragon Mountain

brothers panning for gold in the Jinsha river
attacked by a demon   one was killed
the other fought back with thirteen swords
thirteen peaks above us as we walk
one mountain   one wandering jaggedness

legend's nothing to us   only what's here
for gold one tall sunflower in a field
the mountain points from its Himalayan fold
across the solar system to the other side of the sun
a demon rolls down a slope in the shape of a cloud

no sign though of the sliding river
ice-melt in a high valley paradise
the most southern glacier in the hemisphere
invisible from this track at the end of the village
the wall of swords obscures it

only thoughts can go there   so we walk back
through a place left without events
where voices keep talking into the dusk
in courtyards down through the village street
how to make enough for a tenuous life

one house has a peace sign over the door
my friend shows it me as we pass   as it darkens
what do they fear?   surely
things are easier now? I ask her
but their story   like any other

coils around a secret it protects
various deaths   voices behind walls
the mountain armed   a country
with internal injuries   traces
of blood leaking   doorsteps I can't cross

Protecting the water

passing what looks like a wild cannabis plant
we come to a hut
some beehives   a huge water tank
two old men sit on chairs on a deck

we stop while Xiaomin talks to them
I am asking what creatures live up here
bears   they tell us   *small pandas   snakes*
a special kind of leopard

what are they doing?
protecting the water   she's saying
collected from clouds   running through people
into the poisoned lake   I do not say

on a post is a sign scrawled with characters
two people at a table facing each other
scenes from some alphabet of memory

we go on going down where the path widens
a few geese   two goats   a tea plantation
a sort of kennel-cage where a dog barks

then block after block   rooms for millions
towers of them   a city I can't speak

Lantern festival

from a poem by Xin Qiji (1140–1207)

in one night the east wind brings a thousand trees into blossom
scattering stars around us in bright showers
along the fragrantly flowered roads   cabs drawn by fine horses
fish and dragon lanterns dance through the night
music vibrates from a flute in the full moon

dressed in gold with moth or willow ornaments
in trails of scent young women melt in the crowd
I look for her hearing only their laughter
then all at once   turning my head
I see her there in the soft-shed light of lanterns

I am a dog in a painting by Lowry

not too long-haired or large or floppy   I fit in
always the same kind of people

things to do   places to go
everybody walking everywhere

faces on average kind and full of encouragement
I don't mind though if they ignore me

I love the constant procession towards towards
on we trudge

all have a vision of where they want to get
beyond this street is another that opens

into a space where they gather and where
the numbers are overwhelming

fewer chimneys   more sky   a huge Saturday
who cares about being leashed

Street party July 2016

for the Queen's birthday but postponed
happening now because they want it anyway
the street like a park   cars banned
neighbours sitting around on brought-out chairs

there are games played for generations
one where a line of twos throw eggs to each other
whoever catches one take a step back
as the gap widens eggs fall in the road
eaten by happy dogs

people are throwing sponges of cold water
at two holes cut in a board on stilts
in which faces take turns to get soaked

round the holes   painted portraits   speech-bubbles
one says   *Calm down Boris*
the other   a floss-haired fleeing figure in a suit
mutters   *Time for a quick Brexit*   they love it
now one face is a parent but kids mostly

it takes a street they say to bring up a child
it's true here too   my grandson aged four
out of sight somewhere but people know him
also little Amy having a sulk

there's a guess-who quiz for the inhabitants
I've lived less than a mile away all my life
I have slept in snow caves and igloos
I was born in Seattle in the spring
I sailed to school in the city of the Mary Rose
I am half-Indian half-English

I am a stranger but keep getting introduced
there's a mother from Latvia with her baby
a couple almost forgetting they're splitting up
in this England forgetting it's splitting up

and as night falls and trestles are cleared away
dancing starts   live music
local talent singing Bowie and the Stones
everyone knowing the words
dancing all over the world   and *Brown Sugar*

I see a woman and her twelve-year-old son dancing
she thinking how handsome he is   how he's grown
maybe how it feels to be confidently English
in this happily populated English street
in this affluent fluency   here in Cambridge

Today

The Maiden's round-the-world race   twelve women
reliving it on *Today*

the Southern ocean's storm-force hiss and resistance
finally Portsmouth   a sixty thousand crowd
what's going on?   not thinking it was for them

in a fresh sailing wind with bright flotillas

                                        sunny here too
and the gardener's here   we both go at a years-old thicket
all morning   the lawn strewn   hauling   dragging
burning it by the river   my body aches

a young guy arrives to clean the cooker   brisk
from Rotherham   afterwards tries to sell me a vac cleaner
cordless   big discount
                            lunch-time on impulse
click on a Trump tweet on genes   *well I think I was born*
with the drive for success   I was born with a certain gene

later
in a waiting room for the Pre-diabetes Prevention Programme
A Healthier You at the Community Centre

fill in this please   are you aware of symptoms 0 to10?
                        do you feel loved?   Agree / Disagree
                        satisfied with your life?   more to achieve?

finger pricked for blood-sugar   normal   just above

but there's something worrying me I tell her
whenever I'm writing at night
I need a drink   and e-cigarettes to concentrate
just at night
and once a packet of 20 Chesterfield   smoked three
felt such misery threw the rest in the river
watched as they floated away

in the next room is a singing session
people with learning difficulties   *We are the Champions*
every Thursday somebody does this for them

Black milk

me and my son of sixteen and two Americans
among a thousand square kilometres of trees
in Peru where nights are rapid and sticky

Richard our guide   Nam vet with a '68 killer knife
eyes a deep-set edge in his leathered face

Jack with liver cancer from Missouri   here for a cure
'brought my two sons way back to get laid' he says
'these Iquitos girls…'
aimed at Tom who just feigns interest
thinking instead of catfish   rainbow bass
footsteps away in the lake

and Rodrigo   local village shaman exerting calm
who later heated up pulped vines
psychotria viridis and chacuna
stirring it all up to a black milk

after a day fishing   now it's night
we squat on planks together in a circle
Rodrigo wearing his best black leather jacket

beginning to chant the ritual   what is it?
mixture of church Latin and chewed-up Quechua?

then filling his cheeks with ritual drool
moves between us spraying each in turn

down our necks   in our ears   over our hair
then bringing us his libation cup

I was resistant
swallowing it but thinking of TV antennas
on village huts   screens seen
through banana trees
or the Catholic cathedral packed to the doors
back in Iquitos

and the chanting
like the language of a more ancient spirit
still in the forest   mixed up with half-digested
tracts of communion holiness

what are we doing here
among this loose skin of worn masculinity
but now Richard and Jack are hugging each other

and Rodrigo
even his sprayed drizzle is a kind of care
intimate protection against whatever

but what came out of this sickening sprawling
random jumble of languages
was a vision   afterwards
in the black between my closed eyes
animal faces   jaguar   monkey   python
human   jaguar
hawk   anaconda
each one shading into the next
mouth   nose   snout   jaw
monkey   jaguar   snake   human again

evolution a kaleidoscope
piece by piece appearing in changes
rearranged   reappearing   one vision

then another   the forest itself
both of us heard it   weaving together
frogs   night-jars   buzzings of huge moths
even the gulping and sucking of strange fish
rumblings of poisonous giant toads

above the forest a swarming sound-forest
making a jet-stream high over the canopy
like the gathering dawn sounds of a city

Daily Evolution

the parents divorce
and the father   head of a big local
agricultural merchants

disinherits the son
who becomes nobody
has at last the freedom
of being nobody   but it hurts

that emptiness he carries around
with him in place of a father
trying to be free of it but hurting

working on farms   fighting
fighting it off
asking a question
of this violent town where
nobody is the answer

what hurts now is becoming
somebody   out of nothing
whether he can achieve it
how high are the stakes
and is it worth it?

his mother step-father brother sister
his friends   are all he has
and his ideas   his search
his lively spirit   his doubts

but he is happy   all of these
will be enough to begin with
step by step
works   thrives
writes   hums to himself
this is his daily evolution

go to bed   sleep   dream   keep going
be in the world
keep on being definitely in the world

The least water lily

September heat all day   and out of the car
a cool breeze brushes us from the lake

you start to look for a swimming place
just a few people about
a two-person yacht far off-shore

a notice says this is the home
of the least water-lily   post ice-age flower
the only lake in England where it still lives

you begin your swim   edging
from a spot in the woods into residual ice-melt

the two of you   my daughters-in-law
striking out   laughing because of the cold

maybe I should try searching the margins
for this yellow signal of a survival
still happening whether I find it or not

Husband and wife

curled up inside her hospital nest
a few wisps of feathery hair
a drink   she's saying   *drink*

he feeds her soup then yoghurt from a spoon
a little water
as if soon she'll lift her head
balance it   get stronger

open wide   he says
thank you   she says

there's no sense of an ending between them
just a change of routine
once we did that   now we do this

I have never seen so small a person

one little shift and he opens his eyes
arms jerk out   hands widening to clutch

and I am the unfocused world
any century   any millennia   anywhere

I give him back to his mother and he starts to suck
a long silence

during which species   wonder
become just urgency of the moment

Part Three
Convergent

The story of glass

close to the birth of metals
an instance of something
showered globes   green
in the slag river
brighter than those glazes
on the sarcophagi

no word for it
yet more eyes
waiting for it to appear
thrown from hand to hand
as it cools   accident
of those fires

obscurity inside it almost
shines   like the passage
of daylight through trapped fog
transparency is slow
how long before two mirrors
start to see infinity in each other

fine-ground lenses
close on a cratered moon?
no need for it
in the jagged sky-holes
of Atapuerca   Altamira
pouring in rain   none

until long colonnades
presumed it   columned
spaces   arches   Ionian
flutings   disillusion
with cold   wind   weather
fixing it everywhere

yet how brittle it cracks
caves   hovels
ajar to darkness
then here it is   high towers
panelled by it   passing
the sky between them

Mediterranean

Africa pressed its underground mass towards Europe
shrinking the sea between to a pan of salt

another nudge and sliding ocean poured in
savage tops of mountains become islands

webs of faults   collision after collision   as they arrive
the first people   into a world still in the throes
still quaking   touching it with their footprints

nomads   dark faces
lighting fires on black volcanic sand
lifting oars towards the smudge of an island

a thousand generations of living memory
calling nowhere home
then settlement   wilderness shepherded
where an imagined future stirred underfoot

was it an accident that the middle of the world
found itself   and was founded
where underground weather tumbled rock?

one landslide   one natural massacre
caused people to wonder what power was it
woke them up but too late to prevent it

and soon there were gods   human-like
who could hear you   who knew you
with enough say to chain the monsters of frenzy

faults went on spreading nevertheless
first no wider than a crack in a cup
then jetting mile-high plumes of ash

Herculaneum stared terrified
at what was happening to Pompeii
long before that   Akrotiri
drowned overnight in searing pumice

living with divinity was as treacherous
even the naked Diana implacable
desire changing Acteon to a stag
hunted by his own hounds

Atlas hugely impossible until Perseus
prodding the gorgon's head into his face
seized up his bones into rock still groaning
the sea was still the sea and behaved accordingly
measuring built Atlantis underwater

soon breathing itself became supplication
prayer   ritual   divination   sacrifice
so that everywhere people were doing to animals
what they might have wanted to do to the gods
cut their throats   observe the entrails   study them
then eat the remains

and yet it wouldn't do to distrust them
emanations from clefts   voices of prophecy
events producing shapes before they happened

all those lesser and greater gods
absolute among their mountain heights   beings
so much more beautiful who knew everything

and were out of it   an alternative family
installed in some happy other reality
letting too much wine prevail
over not enough sense
in scenes of just-forgivable havoc

I think of the little town on Keats's urn
its folk that morning
on their way to a grove of olives probably

priest   garlanded beast   various others
the lovers   almost lovers   the kiss   the sacrifice
interrupted

held in a fashioned interlude from time
from what opens under the moment

wild ecstasy   shared at last
surely the gods were present   there forever

while the drift of Africa kept moving
lifting up Olympus by its roots

Hoopoe song

we sit out late and a single hoopoe is calling
caught in a net of myths   bird from the Miocene

the evening sea smooth as the back of a lizard
we drink from ice-rimmed glass

Philomela is a nightingale   Procne a swallow
and the cicadas   who were they before
they became what they are   heat revving the throttle?

a swallow cups the surface of a pool
far off in the valley the dogs howl
at night the hoopoe   calm   loose threads

how good it feels to be changed   says the voice of Tereus
let me not know what I was   let me not know.

Legend of the women of Albion

foremost among the daughters of the King of Greece
Albina the eldest said
we are ourselves not just some man's furrow
should one husband kick against our will
strangle him in bed

so they were all piled in a ship to die   useless with rigging
as with the sea   fell about laughing and cursing life
death   and their youngest sister who went to the King
whispering   *there's a conspiracy   do something!*

they thought of her pillowed while they sprawled
as white palaces changed into rock then cloud
then a storm rose like a fold of lava

the ship drifted north as fate would have it
into its worst capsizing moment
then calm and they were in sight of land

there everything was wild
wild strawberries grew on the cliffs
wild apples fell from the trees   soon to be wild cider

they danced   got merry
and for so long starved of their native Greece
drew from the air beautiful fit black-haired demons to love
bore them children hungry for more love

children of swamps forests mountains mud
caves fires charcoal wolves howling
giants and the incubi of the air

and how long before the arrival of Christ   at whose feet
women became meek   wiping away their tears with their hair
said the legend scratched in parchment Latin

so beware   people of these islands
first of disobedience then the sea   then the air

The weather in Geneva

1816   summer   out on the lake
yet colder than England   a cold wind

just one sail and a rudder fighting the blast
no forecast   sky a coal-black seam
water becoming wilderness as it thrashes

here with her husband and friends
she can't speak
spray spits in her face   they curse God

she sees slabs of exposed mountain
outcrop where a single bolt
causes rock to shout   *I am alive*

they don't know about an eruption
in another place   in a dark hemisphere
jets of ash covering half Europe

afterwards   indoors in a country of rain
they will build a fire and each tell a story

Byron will write 'The Darkness' and Mary
will see a creature running without shelter
its only camouflage the night

I am but what I am I do not know

beggars   thieves   the mad   the lost
jail-filth   brains fresh from the noose

at what point does he become human?
the vacancy in his yellowish eye lustering

he watches weddings   street parties   dancing
all the useful glue that holds them together
skin to skin   kindred to kin   their kindness

the diary of his creator under his coat
draws him towards the secrets of his conception
that his life's a solid lump of want

yet he tries   he must   so much appetite
blood of a rabbit   two wineglasses-worth
fingers wrapping round the neck of a linnet

brows bending lower and lower
studying the force of his own grip

all night in the woods   in mud   in the cold
each day waking smeared   his fluids weeping

spirit   purpose   high sentence
put back furiously in the body
reason running amok in just its shirt

pithecanthropus waiting to be found

Deep in the forest there was a beast

the merchant is determined he's not lost
tired   yet still walking in his own story
wondering who it is owns this forest
sleep stalks him   sleep and dream
a castle with a door and he's pushing it open
into a carved interior   each room lit
not with the dying sun but a fire and bright

surrounding him are tables set for a feast
he serves himself   all he can eat
until morning sleeps in a silken bed
then stepping outside into the garden
drinks the warmth of dawn in a draught
gratefully remembering who he is
his wealth at home untouched   his daughters
it's his youngest though he thinks of most
asking him for a rose

 the rest you know   and when he came back
she was the first to hear it
the rose in his clenched fingers
the theft of it still grafted in his mind
to the Beast's pleasure
that she be exchanged for it
a transaction nothing can now prevent

describe him to me   she says   so he tells her
the cool princely snarl of a man-lion
but prospering   and so will you!
but do you consent?   I do   she said
I will   and soon their carriage
sped through the spring woods

a pheasant crouched underfoot where they dismounted
woodpeckers hammered echoes
but no castle or garden
just travelling with him anguished regret
at an act so foolish and for nothing
or was it nothing?

he pictures a scene of welcome showering them
lavish   unstinting
the lonely host   especially charmed
into pent gestures of generous extremes

and so they go down into deep forest
twisted with passages overgrown and colder

give us some hope   she cried out   we can't go on
this is no story I know   nor how it ends

and staring at her was a man   touching her face
the sound in his throat half-cry   half- voice   brilliant eyes
in amazement wondering what she was
like a child   her high forehead   yet so tall and apart
and she touched him   feeling his skull
its brow ridges fierce like horned armour

where are the long avenues of green architecture
sloping cedars
fountains over ponds of structured water?

this time no door   pushing it open
into a dreamed entitlement
but a long-rumoured horror   human
not- human   from a time when Europe was all forest

the merchant knows at last he has reached the end
and that this creature turning towards him
is itself archaic   aboriginal   as if a lump
of Alpine granite   left by a glacier
commented like a blockage   I am here

he feels his tired heart-rate climb rapidly
into its last hopeless struggle and stand-still

they bury him in the woods
scattering woodland flowers into the grave
where she now casts her rose

from now on she's bonded to sleet and frost
hunger   starlight
ice just inches under the soil
strong-boned heavily weathered faces

she can't tell which of the men painted
in ochre is hers in their stamping dance

in the mornings lies awake hearing speech
in the outside air   blocks of consonant
chipped into sharp vowels

sees tendons in the arms of two young women
stringed instruments worked by fingers
dislocating the body of a flayed deer

sees dawn misting the trees blue-green
then a youth pissing there   so much of it   an arc
the sun transforms to a bright shower
the world still simple to him as a fish-spear
a cluster of little children chirping like sparrows

people wade in the river in a raw wind
skins for covering fastened with the claws of crows
beauty   she whispers   beauty   not knowing why

she wonders how long before history will start
the effort of it slow and clogged with millennia
still hardly inhabited

in the mind of the god she prays to
made in man's image
these people never happened

nothing is left of their deceased lineage
but grave-goods   inarticulate bone
and soon the last vestiges of forest
history will destroy

Tapestry

a greyhound licking his lady's ear
another biting the neck of a deer

fishermen in a boat on the river
a maid   two men   one with a lute

a rearing horse   its upright rider
peasants harvesting stooks

avenue of limes to the house beyond
where a lord and lady in their array

stand as the backdrop of each scene
just as it was and will be

but who's this in the one in Bayeux
head chopped
not knowing whose was the day

then us in ours   stitching   stitched
still in our midst the warp hidden

La Dame de Brassempouy

we can date the ivory but that says nothing
it could have been done by a workman
excavating the site in 1890
carving it in the likeness of his girl

an expert comments in a bar in York
which is the message I email to a friend
living near the place where she was found

I can't let you get away with doubting
its absolute authenticity   he replies
and I accept   wondering though
why it matters who she belongs to
her tribe once?   France?   or to us all?

or a workman   her young neck
high cheek-bones framed by a fall of hair
a face he once held   or never held
his longing making itself ageless

A Wriggle

Time was invisible but with a Wriggle in it
Time was building stars and holes in space
so deep even gravity couldn't escape
such a Wriggle   Time thought   can only die

when it swam loose   Time said   no cause for alarm
this carpet of fossils at Mistaken Point
not one bone among them
two billion years and still nothing with a mouth

Time watched as sets of eyes
popped up from submarine exoskeletons
watched again as worms with legs
started to breathe out of water

and when the Wriggle lurched forward
Time foresaw an immense crater and thought
let's be logical   there are types of incident
we can rely on to clear all this up

eruptions   tar pits   mud slides   floods
Time had them all on its side
and even when the new creature
unclenched its feet and stood erect

Time exclaimed   it's not a problem
we might easily keep it deceived
with ghouls and gods
beings outside of time

this one though had started digging
found little bits of itself and put them together
bones in the hills   wing-traces in shale
almost collapsed in fear but was filled with wonder

and with design   so the moulded face
of an ancestor comes alive   even the cold of stone
against her skin   her thoughts by an ice cliff
inklings of thoughts of those who buried her   by her side
the skull of a deer   a pierced tooth   a bone bracelet

you are my secret
you can't escape
the future is vast
you will die there smeared on the invisible
think you can wriggle out of it?
see me smile   Time said

Bonehead

worlds to come nestled in its synapses   in their long-
                                    withered intricate forest
yet the eyes hold

still gazing at river water twisting among the shoals
each day's passage crossing the current

mouths trying to speak while silt gets drier
itching the sockets

off-shore winds   sandstorms killing the fields

or as one mountain-sized slice of Norway   in a great crash
                                    of subsiding water
tumbles towards Doggerland
still the eyes hold   go on gazing   s their fragile wilderness
                                    collapses
into the catastrophic North Sea

or at the site of Gobekli Tepe   when the first megaliths
                                    emerged
between Turkey and Syria

wind running its fingers through wild wheat
carved tusk of boar   of claw and lion

                        within snarling distance of a volcano
power of rock challenging power of rock

skulls from two million years   the effort of consciousness
trying to fit the ones most suited to it
                                                         dumping the others
across continents
brow ridges becoming eyes helmeted
                                        armies of them sown into the soil

some submitting themselves to alteration   this Aztec
                                                cranium trepanned
in the Archaeology Museum in Lima
                                broken open   mixing mind and sky

or those who will continue the story
fast-flowing with new generations of thoughts   a long trek

crossing grassy plains mountains irrigate   tribes cultivate
herding their cattle
                                gather themselves into their plantations

still the eyes hold   in instant conquest climbing the air
cities at their maximum   crane-high

quake-conscious   calculating the sway
                                        wrap-around balconies and glass

out of flints   knuckles   knots in wood
someone has invented a straight line

so towers of shine mirror each other
rising towards connections of inter-continent

                                                        vapour trails
a skyful of smiling arrows
early morning art-work over London

see themselves finally as they are   a deep-sinking
flutter of skeletal dust   becoming rock

its seams twisted and fractured   still the eyes hold
then gradually not
                                        now as strata
headlands stripped of grass
no longer remembering hair-lines and skin
or the taste of water in cupped fingers

or how they gave each other some ease   so much joy
what wounds they bound or tried to mend

now at one with planets far from the sun   nebulae in folds
                                  where new stars form
caves daylight enters from some other star

Season 1

one year old   learning to walk
      holding on   then letting go

to open arms   total applause
the fall that never happened

you grew up young forever   Mom and Dad
saying your name on the phone
                  to their Mom and Dad
as if it's already in the papers

your wife lifted the lid on your simmering future
then put it back
your kids sprawled on the rug

between you always something
at work   in the air   SPACE the innocent claim
but dangerous

the bitch-goddess   you knew it   *Miss Unspokenof*
silk-white   haunting your nights   sharp as a stiletto
that curve making you want to die

years   and the world has changed around you
no longer yours

Earth is the story now   cyclones fires
flood hunger drought   yet you can't care

after that lift-off nothing comes near

so rapid   so pronounced   to where you are now
trapped in the blast

The night hunters

gory scenes   violence
minds crushed under brow-ridge

then long chords
a major key   consciousness

finding its way
to weightlessness
                guiding itself

deep time scuffed by boot-prints

among animal bones
of the de-fleshed

a playful moment
a spear thrown at the moon

                over the M62

between pylons   wild as the moor skyline

and rising   huge   just as they left it

The fifth age

subtracted from the infinite   human time
weighs hardly a flicker
which is why such divisions have use
four ages   a story   one that measures

so came gold   silver and brass   then iron
each one valuing less   and less valued
greed for power ramping up
to compensate for the loss

people invented power and more power
over the frost the wind the time the flowers

and so the fifth age   you could smell it
the heat-ripple above taxiing aircraft
as they turn up their aim
as power leans back into flight-surge
over a sewage culture of farmed suburbs
utopias of defilement and explosion
huge jets drizzling benzene
into the fires of refineries

was it so wrong to divide up time
into a story set against the invisible   incalculable
one that allowed humans to figure in it?

out of sight of land the shifting ocean
floated in miniature waves between clouds
just as the gods saw it

O Man!   your own hell of a world and the gods against you
judgement imminent   as for punishment
only the worst will suffice but what is it?

Jove spoke   not with a voice   more like a hovering shape

'to them   Nature,'   he said   'is an error
inconvenient   too much wind for their sails   too little
how many thousand years of too much ice   so that now
after so long fixing it   driving through it   over it
ripping its roots out of themselves
just when they think they've conquered   the worst happens
too much heat   too little ice   floods here   there too little water

all we need do is watch in the time left
as they go on trying to correct their corrections
after the drive of iron the ache of bewilderment
complications too many and too great

there's a cure but they'll never find it
the ant-virus virus of an antidote
on and on to infinity   wearing them out

as for stardom   glory   empire   fame
let them go and write their names on fog'

so the gods pondered   crouched together   feet in the sea
hands filling with lava and eruptive dust

'or we could change people into trees
flowers   birds   bushes of myrrh
in place of thoughts the rustling of leaves   leaves
and song   letting bark cover them'

Tracking it

by its scratching-places against trees
little local disturbances of the mud
by how it feeds
where   and the bones scattered

by its path through the overwhelming
forest
by how it runs through gaps   keeping them open
escaping here and there

or by its kindred species still rare
some surviving huge sweepings of cold
out of the ice
by how it has travelled to the four corners

other creatures scattering at its approach
even the fiercest as it walks towards them
all except those in ignorance of it
or those it has tamed

then when we get to it   holed
up in its habitat of every kind
of manufactured detritus   nowhere to go
seeing in its eyes the exhaustion there

pleading with us   with its last breath
for one more chance   promising
it will re-invent itself   with a new skin
will become instead aware and sensitive

to all things living in their plethora of colours
antennae and wings   bugs butterflies
song-birds oceans soil   even the air
everything it has almost completely ravaged

heaving itself up and dropping again
into the terrible waste it had created
churned up by its steel tusks into mud
saying it will reconvene   transform

will we believe it?
searching for a way out of itself
pushed to the limit
crying with the loneliest cry on earth

Going up

glossy book of faces reconstructed
muscled clay sculpted from scanned fragments
moulded into casts   with skin and hair

photo-fits   fronts and sides
staring across 800,000 years
known once only by classified detritus
hand-axes   arrowheads

who knows what it took to shape an edge
grasping both sides of it in your mind?

and what mind?

faces seen like faces in a lift
doors sliding shut on what they're thinking

this Neanderthal old man of forty
eyes like wrinkles in old apple-skin

turn the page
others before him   at a great feast
of vultures   hyenas
scavenging from scavengers

when you look directly into their eyes
is there a gleam you recognise
on its way to becoming who you are?

turn back   two million years
not replicas now but the real thing

you would like to get closer
measure their crania   Broca's area
not from bones of a foot but as they are

and how beautiful they are
scattered together among scattered trees

each one with a hair-line and quick eyes
yet dangerous   this is as near as you dare

your scent breathes on them   strange to them
so they tense and become one single alert
coiling animal

the doors close   and when they open again
we step through
moving out along corridors of glass
towards the distant futures of this building

enclosing us in a world apart
from hunger   weather   how to make fire   skilled

only in living within the controlled confined
static air temperatures of glass

Convergent

Neanderthal bones in a cave at Shanidar
over the plains east of Mosul
its mouth a cry out of the Zagros mountains

speak to us old man skeleton
show us by your arm born withered
by the inflamed burning in ankle and clavicle
by your left eye-socket damaged blind

how from birth your people were your helpers
how tolerance patience courage kindness
aren't just sentiment but necessary

a sixty-thousand- year-old echo and longer
louder than echo even   speak again
from your cave to the city and on and on

sometimes soil is all that's left
the place where a foot was

something touched or breathed-on is enough
fluid seeped from a finger-end

strands from the nuclei of their cells
so that we can say they were here or here

what skull-shape
brain-size   even what empathies they felt

their *now* so hidden and so close
under our feet   no more than a breath away

this lion-man carved in mammoth ivory
music finger-stopped from a swan-bone flute

in the same Europe where on the Elbe
crossing the Rhine   turreted death rode

the tool war making us its species
a future not foretold by a wing-bone's voice

out of Ice Age into this capacity
laying no legible tracks

to this theatre   yet we are here
together an amalgam of joined time

antlers horns wings hands artillery
one being   so many shapes   one story
feeling its way over an open plain

**Part Four
Kerry
Sketches**

On Derrynane Beach

black figure in a wet-suit
playing by the sea's edge
two hundred yards from me
moving further away and further still

a young stranger   not surfing or swimming
just picking up handfuls of water
throwing it back in
there in the fringes   in the displacement
running and jumping   twisting in circles
upright arms in the wind

on the long beach   smaller and smaller
now where the bay curves
to a sandy estuary   vanishes there
so that I found myself willing him to come back
with his surf dance
all the time talking to people around me
as if he'd never existed
and maybe he hadn't

days before   on a beach nearby
an old man came up to me
started talking   no introduction
about a woman he knew who spoke of the sea
as another cosmos touching our own
'even this wind'   he said   'blowing here
comes at us straight out of South America'
then walked off with his dog

I waited for my black figure to come back
was it a disappearance with a return?
then there he was   very far off
coming this way   replacing his absence
back in the story   running again
agile as a seal is underwater

figure from a forgotten myth   seal-human
twisting between
or maybe a casualty from some war
there on the beach he remembered
so much wider than he remembered
back now in life   one of thousands

or it was just his moment of being alone
complete in himself with the pleasure of it
somebody with a name
yards away turning towards me
should I go down to him   speak   say what?
then when I looked again he was gone

I tell it as it was
I went back the next day but he was gone
in the sun the morning sea turquoise
huge beach   tide far out
people scattered across it

Mackerel fishing

Michael the skipper steers his outboard
into the swell and the wind
the sea's three-metre tilt   lash of prow-surf
full in the face   sometimes the boat belly-flops
banging on troughs

then makes the headland
sharp angles of rocks matching the sea's
till an easier lift follows us round
drifting inshore   engine off
thumbs on reels checking the lines down
nothing much coming out
just a few juniors slim as sand-eels

round the head from Derrynane Bay
me Lucy Tom   and Jo his girlfriend
lucky beginner in a no-good season
too many Russian trawlers
but she's the first   three on hers
one on mine   then more and more
Tom shouting to Michael about Norway
where he's just back from
Arctic-sized ones there   great fighters
then nothing   so off again   closer in

fishing   more fishing   thirty   forty
more and more   hugging the cliff
its slant zawns wide-open as caves   so we go in
the sea black-deep in there   so clear
pale seaweed drifting like bones of fingers

then out into rough ocean again
with my son   daughter   all together
salt surf drenching and bucketing
isn't this just the best   I shout to myself
such depths of treacherous chance
after so long bringing me this moment

out to the twin-headed island mostly rocks
drifting into pollock shoals we hope
and they're here   Jo with the biggest of them
our best catch   muscle-streaked sleek-soft
good to eat too   and the next mine
but the prettiest one dad   Lucy said
afterwards on my face the taste of salt

Rip tide

waiting for waves that trigger *go with it*
when it happens ride the accelerations

Jo and Tom with his surf-board while I swim
usual ice-bucket entry over the knees
then with the first roller off my feet

blind swallowing   can't get up or out of it
s*wim swim*   thinking somewhere
beyond these breakers will be a leveller swell

an out-of-my depth feet-on-nothing complicity
with the sea   more than just endurable   peaceful-
seeming   until l sense the beach is too far away
start to make an attempted effort back

but the sea has another plan
while one tide comes it   the other goes out
taking with it anything everything anchorless

I had started to measure my lack of progress
against some just above surface rocks
in a current deceptively unstated

I'd known it before   in rooms   waiting for news
that gradual vanishing of any sign
of respite or escape   and found a way
but this was the sea where worse things happen

desperate   a struggle to the nearest rock
getting somewhere land-like to hold onto
till the weight of a down-plunging wave over it
stripped away any hope that this was help
Tom shouts from a distance   *you alright dad?*
 I don't think I am!   apologetic

seconds later   I thought afterwards
he could have been off on a wave out of range
but is soon with me   then Jo too
each with their calm hurrying instructions

how to construct   still in the sea
some means of resilience using his surf board
hold on   keep going   kick hard

their young lightness   my exhausted heaviness
clawing our way   people watching
as we work at it   stop   breathe   stand up
hug each other   wade back into the dry of the air

Hush little baby don't you cry

Joan Baez's rising and falling voice
on a cd as we drive from the shop
to the old caravan in Brendan's field
how all her trials soon will be over

an extreme so bleak she sings it to God
as we sit eating toasted soda bread
while my two little grandsons wrestle and laugh
giggling together   under the big window
facing the sea   while she sings in my mind

of her brothers   too late for them now
but never mind   in paradise now
with its Tree of Life   her highest strongest note
held like the glittering of a wave
in our paradise with its Tree of Life

Live music night

jammed into the noise
squashed up with friends and others
hearing every third word
what a day it's been   what a summer
almost at the end of it but not yet

live music night   standing room only
spilling into the street the young of all ages
Katy   my daughter's partner
here with her guitar and about to start
everybody now audience

in this same place two years before
an old face at the bar   veteran punisher
waved his claw fist at her   '*English!*
be singing the National Anthem give her the chance
not a doubt'!

tonight though no such interruption
as she begins   the song one of her own
'fly fly away   I don't need you'
tenderly opposing its own words
yet still knowing how love tries us

her voice soaring
alone and strong   reaching the street
while everyone joins in the refrain
accompanied by a man on a tin flute
and a young woman with a violin

Church Island

not for the fishing as it turned out
on this lake by the ocean
just millimetres inland on the map
a salmon and sea-trout stopping place
before they head upward in little rivers
deep into the mountains that surround us

so here we are   casting our lines
into the wind-driven water
one trout to show for it after an hour
in the lee of the island so we go there
eat our lunch in the ruins of the church
just walls   no roof   abandoned remnant

in the middle of the lake
rowing to it   our out-board not working
letting it cool off   for some unplanned
reason now wondering what it was like
for the builders and worshippers
among mountains and water   and the weather

about to come at us out of the West
a deepening trough mixing slopes and rain-bands
and think of them who were the first and last
among these swarms of rain and the hills
with small boats and an abundance of fish
long since gone but an incentive

maybe   along with the pain of it
the atrocity of it   wind and cold rain
each hammering squall's hint of deliverance
each engraved cross a message encrypted
that what must be done will be done
without longing for anything

back on shore   that this was it
trapped between weather and revelation
here at the most exposed point
Atlantic sky attacking windows and doors
its forever arriving lashing downpours
that were the unmerciful moods of God

we can retreat from it   whatever it is
need feel nothing of that savagery
shelter ourselves inside a known
and reliable resistance
managed by our outboard working again
back to this little wharf and landing

Sea life exhibition

propped in one corner a saw-fish beak
single white vertebra of a sperm whale
imagine the rest tapering and tapering

spider-crab carapace you could find
anywhere near here on a lobster run

as if we'd just come upon them ourselves
having to ask what this is or these

this skull's deeply involved ear-duct
horned black handy-sized egg-purses
arm's length jawbone with teeth missing

in this one room how many rooms
how many seas connected to seas?
the raw fact of things as they are

which is why we like this place this way
in deep   unlabelled   out of reach
slipping out of their names

voices signalling each other in the sea
pack-hunters   or for the thrill of it

a one-time chance assembly of strangers
each survival plan's long origin
spawning others like them or unlike

Part Five

**Into the
future tense**

Now we have niche construction technology

for Katy Arnold

your phone opens the door that turns on a lamp
that changes colour to say why the baby is crying

blue for hunger   pink for fever   orange for overtired
the fridge too is signalling *get more milk*
or yoghurt   or freeze-dried coffee

even the walls change colour
telling you your mood before you feel it
technology is telepathy and seamless
no switches so you can't turn it off

phone door walls lamp fridge   even the mirror
each with its need-sensitive sweat-sensor
a thermal device on the baby's wrist

soon everything everywhere will be friendly
considerate   serene
instead of obtuse   maniacal   jagged
the baby hungry and tired   a bit blotchy

parents will forget what they learned by attrition
their entire niche housing the means
the baby itself   before hunger erupts
will begin to pulse blue very quietly

At the lake house

there are some houses from which furniture gradually escapes
an oak desk stands in the yard in the sun
one drawer tightened by wet
this chair still has its legs to stand on
but wood is returning to wood

things seem disinclined to be fixed
towards the lake   beyond the edge of use
all longings for indoor heat and light
freedom from mould and ice
have been abandoned   everything is itself

an old table under the axe cries   I was knot and grain
but you ignored me   with each strike I desert you
your arguments   your cutlery
these splinters are useless except
to the fire which owns me now

rain is filling the lake with jubilations
there will be floods in the margins   changes of colour
at night the creaking of glossed lesions in the woodwork
whispers to the sleepers it's unsafe
they should leave

the days wait behind glass
through the tall woods   voices are echoes
searching for echoes   thoughts
wander   how sometimes   beforehand
things once amazingly were alright

Chimp with frog

La Selva   rippling with thunder
cupped under the Andes

and in a little zoo at the edge of the forest
a chimp holding
a frog to his ear
like a phone

oh evolution   couldn't you
have done something more with him
for him   in the six million years
since we were equals
more than just apish imitation?
loaning him only a frog
without microchip?

why did you not intervene enough
or often enough
to make them both more serious partners
in the big business of bouncing messages
back and forth
to and fro from space
in those times when forest itself
was an eardrum?

why leave the whole thing up to us?

perhaps the message he's listening to
before his phone hops away
is about the vast interconnecting
global and tiny necessity of frog
news now needing instant attention
that can only be said through frog

maybe this is it   truly
what you been trying to tell us all along
that we need something   not just ourselves
to speak through
that otherwise the joke's on us

The natural world

the first things tamed into use were stones
shaping them   accumulating them
following the herds   rivers

sewing together its skinned hides
just to survive the cold of it
burning its wooden bones

knowing yourself by what you will make of it

but not that
having at last found how to subdue it
at your peak   getting us here
after so many millions
of days and nights
you will come face to face with it
in a way never before fathomable

ploughed   shovelled   trampled   with no rights
yet terrible   as when the weight of a wave
thunders towards you
trees howl in their fire-dance

not seeing it except as painted background
deep blue as rock ground into powder
pale blue as eggshells spilling tempera

walking among its forests mountains lakes
amaze us   we say to it   *be strange*   and they are   they do

take me back   show me what it was like
in those fields   in thick snow
making new prints   or in spring   skylarks rising
out of my range eventually

but to its seams   lakes of black
work for us   in furnaces   in the spinning of wheels
towards the limit of its explosions

found hiding inside atoms near Pripyat
where it flies like millions of glowing bullets

walking towards it   where it drops
still in its feathers   dead in your tracks
picked up by a child asking   *who did this?*

Hoxnian

driving through clumps of birch oak hazel
as they were in a dusk similar to this
four hundred thousand years ago

site of some of the earliest tools found
near a lake in the Great Interglacial
now a Suffolk village

how would it be to stop and walk
epochs away from the car   between trees
no different from ghosts of trees?

soon the rising sea will flood inland
rivers become lakes of backed-up water
hardly a finger from the horizon's lip

still I go on thinking this is a wood
a road   traffic   timed by a map
between Norwich and Ipswich

I'm here painting two panels
at a nearby church   Gabriel and Mary
after Fra Angelico's *Annunciation*

but why do it and why you?
you   ask   who like me sense nothing
redemptive in the sea's expanding reach

so that in fifty years of ice melting
he will say his *Ave* underwater

I don't know   is my answer
is bewilderment   learning how the sacred
happened once   or for its beauty

or how the world's reshaped
by massive change
                              in a room
through a window   in our midst
that moment saying her name   her look

Firelight

her mothers and fathers   hearing her breathe
lightly in gasps   wrapped in skins
watch how her eyes watch fire

a stripped-of-leaf deciduous forest
slopes down from mountain-sides to a river

jagged summits   defined on black
harden their ice as a rising moon
sharpens over unmapped streaks of water

while you   also three months
breathe in my arms lightly
alert gaze watching our stove's flames

time is concave   folds them both
that child   this   into one generation
a vulture-bone flute keeps her awake
just as our late talk is your sleep-music

voices and sounds   warm shapes in the air
where tiny hands listen   closing and opening

dying into your life   you into hers
is a movement in nowhere heard by nothing
or is an appearance of more than itself

what protects them   against what
outside the perimeter of firelight?

first the sun made of scatterings of nothing
blown by a wind around it into roundness
then wind in the trees

then fire and the making of fire
into a place of sparks   a centre   an onset

then a story told how this came about   how
even now it could all fly apart   not be at all
yet it still is   it breathes   it has happened

Notes

In the sky with diamonds
some of the initial details here are from an account given in
Donald Johansson and Maitland Edey, *Lucy: The Beginnings of
Humankind* (1981).

Quick brown eyes with something like consciousness
A phrase in Doris Lessing's novel *Shikasta* provided this poem's
title. The first evidence of the use of fire in Britain was from a
site known as Beeches Pit in what is now Thetford Forest.

The Gates of Grief
The Gates of Grief is the name given to the place on the Red Sea
where early hominids, and then our own species, crossed out of
Africa into Asia.

Kathleen
The idea for this poem derives from Wordsworth's 'We are
Seven'.

Anaviapic
The incidents recorded here are from Hugh Brody, *The Other
Side of Eden: Hunter-gatherers, Farmers, and the Shaping of the
World* (2001).

A Legend of Albion
Based on a medieval telling of the founding of Britain.

Hoopoe song
The story of Tereus, his wife Procne and her sister Philomela,
told by Ovid in *Metamorphoses*.

La Dame de Brassempouy
An Upper Palaeolithic sculpture in mammoth ivory, twenty five thousand years old, from the Landes region in south-west France, now exhibited in the Musée de l'archéologie de Saint-Germain-en-Laye.

The fifth age
Written in response to Ovid's account in *Metamorphosis* of the four ages.

Going up
The 'glossy book' referred to is Alice Roberts, *Evolution: the Human Story* (2011).

Hoxnian
The name given to an early interglacial period. The two panels based on Fra Angelico's *Annunciation* are to be installed in the church of St Mary the Virgin, Cratfield, in Suffolk.

Acknowledgements

Sixteen of these poems were first published in the pamphlet *Out of Deep Time* (Wayleave Press 2016), and appear here with thanks to the editor, Mike Barlow. Thanks are also due to the editors of the following publications: *The Compass, Eborakon, The North, PN Review, Stand*; Paul Munden and Shane Strange (eds) *Giant Steps: 21st century poets reflect on the fiftieth anniversary of the Apollo 11 moon landing* (Recent Work Press, 2019), Messa Mahoney and Paul Munden (eds) *Metamorphic: 21st century poets respond to Ovid* (Recent Work Press, 2017), Ian Parks (ed) *Versions of the North: Contemporary Yorkshire Poetry* Five Leaves, 2013).